100+ Fun Ideas for

Teaching French across the Curriculum

in the Primary Classroom

Michelle Williams
and Nicolette Hannam

Brilliant
PUBLICATIONS

We hope you and your pupils enjoy using the ideas in this book. Brilliant Publications publishes many other books for teaching modern foreign languages. To find out more details on any of the titles listed below, please log onto our website: www.brilliantpublications.co.uk.

100+ Fun Ideas for Practising Modern Foreign Languages in the Primary Classroom	978-1-903853-98-6
More Fun Ideas for Advancing Modern Foreign Languages in the Primary Classroom	978-1-905780-72-3
Chantez Plus Fort!	978-1-903853-37-5
Hexagonie 1	978-1-905780-59-4
Hexagonie 2	978-1-905780-18-1
Jouons Tous Ensemble	978-1-903853-81-8
C'est Français!	978-1-903853-02-3
J'aime Chanter!	978-1-905780-11-2
J'aime Parler!	978-1-905780-12-9
French Pen Pals Made Easy	978-1-905780-10-5
Loto Français	978-1-905780-45-7
French Festivals and Traditions	978-1-905780-44-0
Bonne Idée	978-1-905780-62-4
Unforgettable French	978-1-905780-54-9
¡Es Español!	978-1-903853-64-1
Juguemos Todos Juntos	978-1-903853-95-5
¡Vamos a Cantar!	978-1-905780-13-6
Spanish Pen Pals Made Easy	978-1-905780-42-6
Lotto en Español	978-1-905780-47-1
Spanish Festivals and Traditions	978-1-905780-53-2
Buena Idea	978-1-905780-63-1
Singt Mit Uns	978-1-905780-78-5
Das ist Deutsch	978-1-905780-15-0
Wir Spielen Zusammen	978-1-903853-97-9
German Pen Pals Made Easy	978-1-905780-43-3
Deutsch-Lotto	978-1-905780-46-4
German Festivals and Traditions	978-1-905780-52-5
Gute Idee	978-1-905780-65-5
Giochiamo Tutti Insieme	978-1-903853-96-2
Lotto in Italiano	978-1-905780-48-8
Buon'Idea	978-1-905780-64-8

Written by Nicolette Hannam and Michelle Williams
Illustrated by Catherine Ward
Editorial, design and production by Bookcraft Ltd
Front cover illustration Kate Shannon
Cover designed by Brilliant Publications

Printed ISBN: 978-1-905780-79-2
Ebook ISBN: 978-0-85747-134-5

First printed and published in the UK in 2010

Published by Brilliant Publications
Unit 10
Sparrow Hall Farm
Edlesborough
Dunstable
Bedfordshire
LU6 2ES, UK
Email: info@brilliantpublications.co.uk
Website: www.brilliantpublications.co.uk
Tel: 01525 222292

The name Brilliant Publications and the logo are registered trademarks.

Contents

Introduction

This book was written by Michelle Williams, a primary school teacher, and Nicolette Hannam, a secondary school teacher. While team-teaching French to Year 5 they looked at classroom displays, and began to see how easily French could be accommodated within normal lessons and embedded across the curriculum. This approach to language learning is known as Content Language Integrated Learning (CLIL).

The authors spent time examining the National Curriculum and identifying places where a link with French was possible. After much planning, teaching and evaluating they have now refined their ideas and collected them in this book, aimed at supporting schools that have chosen French as a modern foreign language for pupils throughout Key Stage 2.

How does CLIL work?

CLIL involves teaching a subject, such as history or maths, in the target language, where possible. It encourages a dual-language approach to any chosen topic, embedding the language within other subjects, and so enhancing pupils' learning across the curriculum.

CLIL lessons can be stimulating and challenging. They are most successful when they are supported by visual aids, such as flashcards or dual-language interactive whiteboard presentations. Tasks should support pupils by reinforcing prior language knowledge and introducing new vocabulary gradually. These tasks often provide material for excellent creative displays that link work across the curriculum, helping pupils to retain information.

Why is CLIL beneficial?

The benefits of using a CLIL approach to lessons are many. Pupils can engage with a new language while also gaining knowledge in the target subject area. They are highly motivated by CLIL lessons, and enjoy this way of learning, as they are using their new language for a real purpose. Teachers have the opportunity to experience higher levels of job satisfaction, and develop innovative examples of good practice to share with other teachers.

CLIL lessons can further develop children's cultural knowledge and understanding. They will improve children's confidence in their language learning, and their communication skills.

Many teachers find the prospect of teaching French a little daunting and have visions of spending hours planning new and exciting lessons. But CLIL lessons make best use of curriculum time and give pupils extra time with their target language. Instead of competing for crucial teaching and learning time, CLIL allows French to complement other lessons. Over time a school will reap the rewards of using CLIL across the curriculum, and feel proud of the motivation and success of its learners.

Tips for introducing the teaching of French through CLIL

✦ As with all new initiatives, introduce plans for CLIL teaching gradually.

✦ Start by assessing teachers' prior knowledge and levels of confidence – perhaps through a questionnaire.

✦ Plan clear steps, and make sure these are communicated clearly to other teachers.

✦ Make sure you provide a high level of support to staff.

✦ Evaluate plans that have been put into practice and adapt future plans as appropriate, taking all opinions into account.

✦ Offer to work with year groups to help identify places where French could be used to introduce and reinforce new subject knowledge; plan lessons together, ensuring coverage of the curriculum. Look on the Brilliant Publications website (www.brilliantpublications.co.uk) for charts showing how the activities in this book link to the National Curriculum.

✦ Talk with other staff about how to support children who have difficulties.

✦ Plan careful use of resources: which visual aids will be available, when, and to whom?

✦ Discuss with other staff what expectations you all have about final outcomes of this way of teaching.

✦ Model some CLIL teaching for other staff to watch.

✦ Share successes with other staff.

Activities that work particularly well in a CLIL lesson

✦ Making simple oral responses to key questions and statements. For example, ask children to respond to statements with either 'true' or 'false' ('vrai' or 'faux').

✦ Ordering information: for example, putting in order pictures and sentences showing scenes from a play or fairytale.

✦ Following simple instructions on a regular basis: for example, when warming up for PE.

✦ Using Loop cards: children have a card showing both a question and an answer. One child starts by reading out their question, and the child with the answer on their card reads out the answer, then poses the next question – and so on.

✦ Carrying out class surveys using questionnaires, the results to be recorded in French.

✦ Playing guessing games, such as Twenty Questions. One child thinks of an object and the other children ask questions, trying to narrow down the possibilities until they can identify the mystery object.

Using CLIL alongside other French teaching

CLIL is an excellent way of engaging children and teachers, but it is not sufficient. Children will need access to dedicated French lessons when they focus specifically on French vocabularyand simple sentence structures. These lessons should be interspersed with regular CLIL lessons to further stimulate and enhance the children's learning across the entire curriculum.

English

Speaking and listening skills feature in every French lesson as children read out loud, question each other, take on roles and discuss meanings of words. These skills can be successfully transferred to English lessons. Using French can reinforce understanding of the rules of English as children make crucial comparisons of language and spelling between the two languages.

Guided reading sessions can sometimes involve simple French texts, with children picking out key words. Ask children to find examples of questions, and identify the answers.

Writing can be modelled in French for the children to use as support. Punctuation can be reinforced whilst writing in French. Older children can be asked to punctuate a simple French text.

Speaking and listening

Speaking

1. Learning good habits

✦ Tell children you are going to demonstrate both good and bad speaking habits. Do so, then discuss and clarify the differences.

✦ Discussion topics: what happens if you don't look at the person you are speaking to? How does it make the other person feel? What is your body language saying? How should you react when someone doesn't look at you while talking to you?

✦ Take some photographs and display them as a reminder to children about what good verbal communication looks like.

2. Reading and speaking aloud

✦ Reading aloud is only required at a very basic level, but practising little and often will help children improve steadily.

✦ Model phrases and sentences for the children to repeat as a whole class. They could repeat key phrases from a traditional story, or have a key phrase to say every time a character is mentioned.

✦ Show children a clip of French children reading their work aloud, and discuss their delivery.

✦ Assess children's levels of fluency, comprehension and enjoyment.

3. Using big books

✦ Use French big books to add variety in literacy lessons – either real books or CD-ROMs with an interactive whiteboard. As you read aloud, the children join in where they can. Highlight some phrases for all the children to try, with a lot of praise as they have a go.

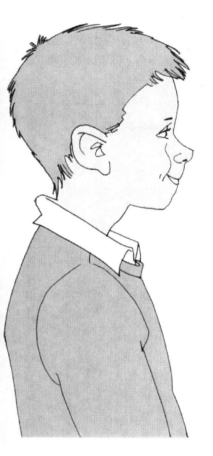

✦ Ask comprehension questions about the big book for children to answer verbally. Use both open and closed questions, and questions that require inference and deduction skills.

4. Presenting to different audiences

✦ Give children opportunities to speak in French to a range of audiences: each other, teachers, parents, other classes ...

✦ Use a wide variety of role-play in pairs and in small groups so children get practice in taking on different roles and talking to different kinds of people.

5. Play reading

✦ Help a group of children to read or perform a simple play based on a traditional story such as *L'Histoire des Trois Petits Cochons* (*The Three Little Pigs*).

L'Histoire des Trois Petits Cochons

List of characters

Narrateur	*Narrator*
Le Petit Cochon 1	*Little Pig 1*
Le Petit Cochon 2	*Little Pig 2*
Le Petit Cochon 3	*Little Pig 3*
Le Grand Méchant Loup	*The Big Bad Wolf*

Narrateur

Il était une fois Trois Petits Cochons.

Once upon a time there were Three Little Pigs.

Un matin, ils ont quitté la ferme pour construire chacun une maison.

One morning they left the farm to build their own houses.

Le Petit Cochon 1

Je vais construire ma maison en paille.

I'm going to build my house from straw.

Narrateur

Donc, il a construit sa maison en paille.

So he built his house from straw.

Alors le Grand Méchant Loup s'est approché et il a frappé à la porte.

Then, the Big Bad Wolf came and knocked on the door.

Le Grand Méchant Loup

Gentil Petit Cochon, est-ce que je peux entrer?

Nice little pig, may I come in?

Le Petit Cochon 1

Mais non, mais non. Pas par les poils de mon petit menton, tu ne peux pas entrer.

No, no. Not by the hair on my chinny, chin, chin.

Le Grand Méchant Loup

Alors, je vais souffler encore et encore pour abattre ta maison.

Then I'll huff and I'll puff till I blow your house down.

Narrateur

Donc il a soufflé encore et encore et la petite maison s'est envolée. Puis il a dévoré le Petit Cochon.

So he huffed and he puffed and he blew the house down. Then he ate the Little Pig.

Le Petit Cochon 2

Je vais construire ma maison en bois.

I'm going to build my house from wood.

Narrateur

Donc, il a construit sa maison en bois.

So he built his house from wood.

Le Grand Méchant Loup s'est approché et il a frappé à la porte.

Then, the Big Bad Wolf came and knocked on the door.

Le Grand Méchant Loup

Gentil Petit Cochon, est-ce que je peux entrer?

Nice little pig, may I come in?

Le Petit Cochon 2

Mais non, mais non. Pas par les poils de mon petit menton, tu ne peux pas entrer.

No, no. Not by the hair on my chinny, chin, chin.

Le Grand Méchant Loup

Alors, je vais souffler encore et encore pour abattre ta maison.

I'll huff and I'll puff till I blow your house down.

Narrateur

Donc il a soufflé encore et encore et la petite maison s'est envolée. Puis il a dévoré le Petit Cochon.

So he huffed and he puffed and he blew the house down. Then he ate the Little Pig.

Le Petit Cochon 3

Je vais construire ma maison en brique.

I'm going to build my house from bricks.

Narrateur

Donc, il a construit sa maison en brique.

So he built his house from bricks.

Le Grand Méchant Loup s'est approché et il a frappé à la porte.

The Big Bad Wolf came and knocked on the door.

Le Grand Méchant Loup

Gentil Petit Cochon, est-ce que je peux entrer?

Nice little pig, may I come in?

Le Petit Cochon 3

Mais non, mais non. Pas par les poils de mon petit menton, tu ne peux pas entrer.

No, no. Not by the hair on my chinny, chin, chin.

Le Grand Méchant Loup

Alors, je vais souffler encore et encore pour abattre ta maison.

Then I'll huff and I'll puff till I blow your house down.

Narrateur

Donc il a soufflé encore et encore et encore et encore et encore …

So he huffed and he puffed and he huffed and he puffed and he huffed and he puffed …

Mais la grande maison en brique ne s'est pas envolée.

But the house made from bricks didn't fall down.

Le Grand Méchant Loup

Alors, je vais descendre par la cheminée pour manger le Petit Cochon.

Then I'll climb down the chimney to eat the Little Pig.

Le Petit Cochon 3

Je vais mettre une marmite à bouillir pour préparer mon dîner.

I'll put a pot on the fire to prepare my dinner.

Narrateur

Le Grand Méchant Loup est tombé dans l'eau chaude. Il a sauté hors de la marmite et il s'est échappé de la maison!

The Big Bad Wolf fell into the hot water. He jumped out of the pot and escaped from the house!

6. **Asking and answering questions**

✦ To revise and reinforce words, use quick fire questions in French. Encourage every child to answer at least one question.

✦ Ask each question at least three times, and remind children to listen to the answers. Less confident children will hear the answer modelled before having a go themselves.

✦ Use hot-seating with characters from stories or people from non-fiction texts – in French. The teacher, or a child, takes the hot seat and invites questions from the audience.

✦ Use a set of flashcards with words from any area of the curriculum (for example, names of mountains or rivers). Children ask you questions to try to identify which one is top of the pile.

Listening

7. Following a story that is read aloud

✦ Read a French version of a familiar story. Teach children actions, or key words, for parts of the story. This encourages everyone to participate and makes the story easier to follow.

✦ With multiple user licenses for websites and plenty of headphones children can listen to stories on computers. This allows individuals to progress at their own rate.

8. Conversing with a visitor from France

✦ Pretend to be a visitor from France. Explain in very simple terms who you are or what you do (are you a baker, a teacher, an astronaut … ?) and invite children to ask you questions. This activity could lead to a report for a school newspaper or an assembly.

✦ Focus on an area of France and encourage questions about culture and traditions. Sensitively, help children compare these to their own traditions.

9. Paying attention to pronunciation and spelling

✦ Remind children to listen carefully to how words are pronounced in French and to try to speak as accurately as possible. Model pronunciation yourself, if confident, or use websites or CD-ROMs.

✦ Look at some English words with tricky spellings. Explain how to say these words to a French person.

✦ Build word banks of words with tricky spellings/ pronunciations in both languages.

✦ Children use small microphones to record themselves speaking in French. When they play back their recordings they evaluate their own pronunciation. Listen with them and help them to identify which words still sound as if spoken by an English person. How does the child need to change their pronunciation?

✦ Give children opportunities to examine the written word and compare it to the spoken word. For example, they could build a bank of French words where the last letter(s) are not heard. Can they think of any similar instances in English?

10. Adapting your voice to the purpose of the text

✦ Look at some text in French – for example a recipe. Discuss with children how to tell that it is a recipe. Together, read it out, adapting your tone of voice accordingly.

✦ Discuss other purposes of text – to persuade, instruct, entertain ... . Look at some samples and ask the children to highlight the features that tell them what kind of text it is. Decide on a suitable tone of voice for reading it out.

11. What to say when you don't understand

✦ Give children phrases to use when they don't understand a question or instruction.

Répétez s'il vous plaît.	*Please repeat that.*
Je ne comprends pas.	*I don't understand.*

Group discussion and interaction

12. Taking turns appropriately

✦ When children practise role play, remind them to take turns. Talk about body language, focusing on how to indicate you want a turn to speak, and how to tell when someone wants to speak.

✦ Give out roles: the blushing flower, the dominant person, the hesitant person, the peacemaker ... . The group must decide what kind of outing to choose if they had a day out in France. After 5 minutes, swap roles around so that children take on a different persona. Continue with the discussion about the outing: what kind of transport will they use, and what kind of meal will they have?

13. Giving explanations

✦ Challenge confident children by asking them open questions about themselves (in role or as their real selves). Encourage them to explain themselves in detail.

Teacher	As-tu des frères et des soeurs?
Pupil	Oui, j'ai une soeur.
Teacher	Décris-moi ta soeur.
Pupil	Elle s'appelle Amy.
Teacher	Quel âge a-t-elle?
Pupil	Elle a douze ans.
Teacher	Très bien. Maintenant, encore une fois. As-tu des frères ou des soeurs?
Pupil	Oui, j'ai une soeur qui s'appelle Amy. Elle a douze ans.

14. Conventions of politeness

✦ Encourage children to use good manners in French lessons. Teach them to say 'Merci' as soon as they learn the basics.

Ça va?

Oui, ça va bien, merci. Et toi?

15. Role-play

✦ Give children lots of opportunity to role-play different characters. They could be shop keepers, postal workers, café attendants – whatever fits in with your topic of the moment.

✦ Sometimes, give children a basic script to work with. Confident children can add their own ideas.

✦ As a follow up to role play, children take a 'hot seat' and pretend to be a character from the play. The audience ask questions in French. Opposite are some ideas for general questions and answers relating to characters in traditional tales.

16. Conveying emotion

✦ Learning to convey emotion can start with answering one of the first questions learnt in primary French – *Comment ça va?* With the children, consider suitable actions and facial expressions to go with different answers.

✦ Encourage children to speak with expression, for example, raising the tone of their voice at the end of questions.

Possible questions	Possible answers
Comment t'appelles-tu?	Je m'appelle ...
As-tu des frères et des soeurs?	J'ai un frère/deux frères. J'ai une sœur/deux sœurs. Je suis fils unique/Je suis fille unique.
As-tu un animal?	J'ai un chat/J'ai un chien.
Où habites-tu?	J'habite dans le bois.
Quelle est la date de ton anniversaire?	Mon anniversaire, c'est le dix janvier.
Qu'est-ce que tu aimes manger?	J'aime les fruits et le chocolat.
Quel est ton passe-temps préféré?	J'aime le foot./J'aime la danse.
Quel temps fait-il dans le bois?	Il pleut/Il y a du soleil/Il neige.
Qu'est-ce que tu portes?	Je porte un jean et un sweat.

Standard English/French

17. Formal and informal language choices

✦ Tell children that in France there are two different ways to say 'you.' In a formal situation or with someone you don't know, you use *vous*. In an informal situation or with people you know, use *tu*.

Comment t'appelles-tu?

Comment vous appelez-vous?

✦ Discuss whether there are similar conventions in English. Do we have different ways of saying 'you'? Do we use formal and informal ways of addressing people, depending on our relationship with them ?

Language variation

18. **Exploring dialect**

◆ Tell children that the official language of France is French, but there are many regional dialects such as Basque, Breton, Catalan and Provençal.

◆ Discuss what children know about dialect. Can they name, or use, any dialects used in Britain? Can they give examples of how vocabulary varies depending on where in the country you come from?

◆ This could lead on to a discussion of why Standard English is used as a common language, available to all, in newspapers, books and on television.

Dialects spoken in France

Basque is spoken in north-eastern Spain and south-western France.

Breton language is a Celtic language spoken in Brittany.

Provençal dialect is spoken in the South of France.

Catalan is spoken on both sides of the eastern part of the Pyrenees Mountains.

---

19. Reading familiar phrases aloud

✦ Make a display of questions for children to refer to when conversing in French, in role play or hot seating. Read through these with children occasionally to help them to develop their fluency.

Possible questions	Possible answers
Comment ça va?	Ça va bien, merci.
Comment t'appelles-tu?	Je m'appelle Daniel.
Quel âge as-tu?	J'ai sept ans.
Quelle est ta couleur préférée?	J'aime le noir/gris/marron/ jaune/rouge/rose/blanc/ violet/bleu.
As-tu un animal?	Oui, j'ai un chien. Non, je n'ai pas d'animal.
As-tu des frères et des soeurs?	Oui, j'ai deux frères et une soeur.
Quelle est la date de ton anniversaire?	C'est le vingt-neuf juin.
Où habites- tu?	J'habite à Mirfield.
Quel temps fait-il?	Il fait beau./Il pleut.
Qu'est-ce que tu aimes faire?	J'aime le foot./J'adore la natation.

20. Using bilingual texts

✦ Pair up a younger and an older child to read a bilingual book together – for example, a Year 3 child reads the English text out loud, and a Year 6 child reads the corresponding French.

21. Using French texts

✦ Collect French holiday brochures for reading with children. Together work out some meanings of words and phrases.

✦ Look at a range of other kinds of text, including poems, nursery rhymes, fairy tales and stories and ask children to scan them for words they know. How much of the meaning can they obtain? Compare the text with the English equivalent, and try to match words.

22. Looking at features of non-fiction texts

✦ Reinforce typical features of non-fiction text by looking at a French non-fiction book. Give children a photocopied page and ask them to highlight any features they notice: headings, sub-headings, diagrams, pictures and captions, and so on. They should be able to do this despite not understanding the majority of the text.

23. Learning about parts of speech

✦ To reinforce children's understanding of nouns, adjectives and verbs in English, get them to examine simple French sentences and highlight the different parts of speech.

KEY	Le **chien** bleu *est* féroce.
adjective	Le **hamster** rouge *est* énorme.
noun	Le petit **singe** *est* rigolo.
verb	J'*aime* les **chips**.

✦ This creates an ideal opportunity to discuss and compare word order in both languages.

Writing

24. Writing for real-life situations

✦ Provide real-life situations where children need to compose various text types: writing to pen pals, using an informal letter style, writing a piece to read out in assembly or to display in the school hall, writing an invitation to another class to join in a French lesson/game/meal.

25. Writing for invented situations

✦ Provide invented situations where children need to compose various text types:

  ✦ writing an information text about Paris

  ✦ writing a diary, pretending to be on holiday in France

  ✦ writing a newspaper article about a special event, such as a French Day held in school.

✦ Encourage children to plan briefly, and then draft their work. They should recognize the benefits of this, and produce a final piece of work that is of high quality.

26. Practising punctuation

✦ Remind children that punctuation matters in French just as it does in English. Ask children to redraft any sentences where the punctuation is unacceptable.

27. Focusing on spelling

✦ Give each pair of children a sheet of paper. Read out a list of words for pairs to discuss and write down. They then swap with another pair and mark answers as you call them out.

✦ Use flashcards to display the written words. Pairs score one point for a good try, two points if the word is spelt correctly, and an extra point for getting the article (*le*, *la* or *les*) correct.

✦ Children collect French words with similar spelling patterns, or similar sounds. For example:

  vin, magasin, lapin, poussin

28. Looking at handwriting

✦ If possible, show children some handwriting done by a French child. Handwriting expectations are very high in France, and schoolchildren practise until they can 'join up' beautifully. Children could practise writing their names in a similar script.

29. Considering degrees of formality

✦ When children write to their pen pals there is an opportunity to reinforce their understanding of the use of Standard English. Discuss the informality of their letter. How do you know it is informal? How could you change this to a more formal letter? When do you use an informal or a formal tone?

30. Language structure

✦ Language structure only needs examining at a basic level in French, but it can be used to reinforce understanding of the English language. Remind children what nouns, verbs, adjectives and adverbs are. When translating simple sentences, talk about changing the word order where necessary.

✦ Explain the use of the articles *le, la* and *les* and *un, une, des* and talk about how they often determine the spelling of any adjective.

> *Le poussin jaune est petit* (not *petite*).
>
> *Je porte une grande veste bleue* (not *bleu*).

Maths

Children really enjoy counting in French, even singing the numbers back to their teacher. Once they have learnt the numbers, they can use them to do simple calculations, such as number bonds to ten or twenty, and to work on oral problems – all in French. It will make lessons more fun and move the focus from practising maths to reinforcing language skills. Children will improve their maths without even noticing.

Number

Using and applying number

31. Solving word problems

✦ Pose simple word problems linked to topics they are learning about in French. For example:

> *Josh mange cinq pommes et Hannah mange sept pommes. Ça fait combien?*
>
> *Ella a trois chats et Joel a deux chats. Ça fait combien?*

✦ Ask children to highlight the key words, especially those which indicate what operation to use. They may also choose to cross out information that is not useful.

✦ Ask children to write some similar problems for a friend or pen pal to solve, based on the same model.

Numbers and the number system

32. Counting

✦ Regularly count with children, in French, from 1–10 and back then from 1–20 and back. If you incorporate actions or movements for each number, this can help them remember the words.

✦ Older children could count in tens to 100, and back again; or to 1 000 in hundreds.

33. Playing 'Guess the number'

✦ One player chooses a number in secret, which the class then try to guess. The Chooser gives clues until the class have found the target number.

Vingt?	Twenty?
C'est moins.	It is less.
Dix?	Ten?
C'est plus.	It is more.

34. Sequencing numbers

✦ When working with number sequences, offer double points if children can give the next number in French.

✦ Practise counting in twos, fives or tens in French. Children could march or clap to keep a steady rhythm.

35. Spelling out number words

✦ When children learn to spell the French numbers to 20, suggest they draw pictures of objects to match. They could choose their own theme to personalize their learning.

✦ Give children a pair of numbers written as words in French. They write them out, adding the appropriate more than/less than symbol (< or >) between them.

deux < neuf

36. Having fun with fractions

✦ To make fractions fun and French, share out some French food. Make or buy some galettes or a brioche, and talk with the children about the different ways in which you could cut them. Take photographs to use in a cross-curricular display.

37. Linking decimals with money

✦ Talk about a penny as being worth 1/100 of a pound, and establish the notation for writing English money. Talk about how Euros and cents follow a similar system. Children write prices for some traditional French items in Euros and cents, then put them in order. Ask them to say the value of each digit.

✦ Write up a list of decimal numbers. Children round each to the nearest whole number and give the answer in French.

Calculations

38. Operating on numbers

Read out simple calculations in French for children to do. It can help to provide a poster showing the mathematical operations in French.

plus	*plus/add*
moins	*subtract/take away*
fois	*multiply*
divisé par	*divided by*
égal	*equals*

39. Using calculators

✦ Children may use calculators to help them solve problems using large numbers. Such problems can be based on facts about France, using Euros and items in French shops.

✦ Get children to share a calculator. One partner uses the calculator, but may only press the keys as instructed by the other partner. All this to be done in French, of course.

Simpler problems

La Boulangerie baked 672 croissants and sold 543. How many did they have left at the end of the day?

The EuroStar train leaves London and travels 135 km to Dover. It then travels 50 km in the Eurotunnel, and 296 km from Calais to Paris. How far is the total journey from London to Paris?

Trickier problems

The highest mountain in The Pyrenees is Aneto at 3 404 m. A smaller mountain is Pic d'Anie at 2 504 m. What is the difference between their heights?

There are 1 665 steps to the top of The Eiffel Tower. If it takes 30 seconds to climb 10 steps, and you keep climbing at the same speed, how long will it take to climb to the top?

Solving numerical problems

40. Numerical and word problems

✦ Give children co-ordinates in French to plot on a graph.
Choose co-ordinates so that joining them forms a picture
of the Eiffel Tower or the Louvre.

✦ Children can design a picture of a French object or place,
and give the co-ordinates to a partner to see if they can
draw the picture accurately.

Shape, space and measures

Using and applying shape, space and measures

41. Working with clocks

✦ Help children to learn to say the time in French. This will reinforce their understanding of clock time.

✦ Start a lesson with children holding small clocks and showing the times that you call out in French. As their understanding develops offer more challenging activities.

✦ Children draw the hands on a clock to match a time written in French words, then write the time, in French, to match their clock.

✦ Challenge children with a list of times written in English and another in French and ask them to pair them up correctly.

42. Learning the 24-hour day

✦ Children write the time, in words, as shown on a 24-hour clock.

19:54

43. **Timetables and schedules**

✦ Children pretend to be on holiday in France and plan a day, detailing the times.

✦ Give children problems about French timetables or television schedules, based on real information from the internet. For example, a bus that should have arrived at 10.15 am is twenty minutes late; when does it arrive?

Time vocabulary

Il est six heures	*Six o'clock*
Il est six heures et demie	*Half past six*
Il est six heures et quart	*Quarter past six*
Il est six heures moins le quart	*Quarter to six*
Il est six heures vingt-cinq	*Twenty-five past six*
Il est sept heures moins vingt	*Twenty to seven*

Understanding properties of shape

44. Naming shapes

Ask children to draw a shape on their whiteboards or in the air, according to the word you say in French. They could then label the vertices and right angles.

un cercle	*circle*
un carré	*square*
un rectangle	*rectangle*
un triangle	*triangle*
un pentagone	*pentagon*
un hexagone	*hexagon*
un heptagone	*septagon*
un octogone	*octagon*

✦ Add a colour word and ask the children to draw what you describe.

un triangle bleu	*a blue triangle*
un cercle rouge	*a red circle*
un carré jaune	*a yellow square*
un rectangle vert	*a green rectangle*

45. Examining shapes

✦ Children count aloud in French as you touch the sides, vertices, or right angles of a shape shown on the whiteboard.

✦ Use a feely bag. As children reach in and feel the shape they say the name in French.

✦ *C'est un triangle.*

✦ Older children could give a reason for their guess.
C'est un triangle parce qu'il a trois côtés.

Understanding properties of position and movement

46. Drawing treasure maps

✦ Children draw a treasure map on squared paper and use co-ordinates, in French, to direct a friend to the treasure.

✦ To develop their knowledge of the wider world, use a map of France for this, and draw a co-ordinate grid on top of it.

47. Playing Battleships

✦ Children label a squared grid and use it to play Battleships in French. (For full instructions on how to play, look on the internet.)

✦ Vary the basic game by linking it to a topic you are exploring in French, such as furniture or buildings. Children draw five objects (a chair, a table, a rug ...) in squares on their copy of the grid, making sure their partner can't see their grid. They name various co-ordinates in French, asking whether the named square has a piece of furniture on it. The first player to find out or 'hit' all five of their partner's objects is the winner.

touché	hit
coulé	sank
manqué	miss
presque	close
Oui, tu as touché la chaise	Yes, you have hit the chair
Non, tu as raté	No, you missed

Understanding measures

48. **Opening a French shop**

✦ Open a French shop in your classroom, with typical French food. Label the items for sale with their weight or capacity. Ask questions about these in English (answers to be given in French where possible).
How much juice is there in this carton?
Which is the heavier/lighter of these two tins? What is the difference in weight between them?
Can you find three items whose weight totals 1.5 kg? How many grams is that?

49. **Including prices**

✦ Put price labels on the items in your French shop – in Euros. Again, ask questions about these in English.
Which is the most expensive item in the shop? Which is the cheapest?
What is the difference in price between these two items?

✦ Choose two items to buy. Can you pay for them with a 20€ note? How much change will you get?

Handling Data

Using and applying handling data

50. Using tally charts

✦ One group of children asks others in the class what their favourite colour is and records the answers in a tally chart.

Quelle est ta couleur préférée? J'aime le bleu.

✦ Other groups carry out a similar survey with pets or siblings.

As-tu un animal? *Oui, j'ai deux chiens.*

As-tu des frères et des soeurs? *Oui, j'ai une soeur.*

✦ Ask children to outline their results in French.

Dix enfants aiment le bleu.

Trois enfants aiment le jaune.

Cinq enfants ont un chien.

51. Conducting a holiday survey

✦ Children carry out a survey of where in France they have been on holiday, or where they would like to go. Discuss the best way of recording information as it is collected, and whether to present the data in a tally chart, a line or a bar graph.

✦ Display the results next to a map of France or Europe. Label the main places chosen by the children, and some of these places' features, helping children to pronounce these words correctly.

Processing, representing and interpreting data

52. Using Venn diagrams

There are many ways of using Venn diagrams in language lessons – for example, when comparing festivals and traditions. Use a Venn diagram to record similarities and differences between birthday or Easter celebrations in Britain and France.

✦ Use a Venn diagram to sort French and English words. This makes clear which words are spelt the same in both languages.

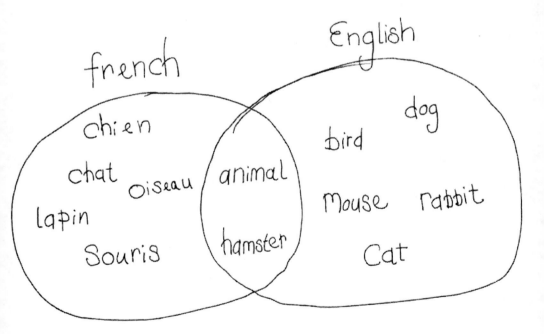

53. Using Carroll diagrams

✦ Use Carroll diagrams to reinforce understanding of map
work, for example:
Towns in France/not in France
French towns on the coast/not on the coast

54. Incorporating French into all kinds of work

✦ Use French for cross-curricular displays on any topic.
Add key French vocabulary or facts to a display on
weather. Include examples of written French in a display
of best handwriting. Ideas are limitless. You could
challenge yourself to include something from the foreign
language curriculum in each of your displays. Can the
children spot it?

Science

✦ There are many opportunities in science to incorporate key words in French. Children will enjoy calling out in French in response to a prediction. After an investigation they can say in French whether or not they agree with another group's conclusion.

✦ Add key French words to displays, with key questions, to demonstrate the extent of the children's cross-curricular learning.

Scientific enquiry

Carrying out enquiries

55. Measuring and reading scales

✦ Occasionally, challenge children to state measurements in French.

C'est trente-deux centimètres.

C'est quarante grammes.

56. Making comments

✦ Teach children simple sentences stating whether or not a test is fair.

Oui, c'est juste.

Non, ce n'est pas juste.

✦ Or saying whether or not they agree with another group's findings.

Oui, nous sommes d'accord.

Non, nous ne sommes pas d'accord.

✦ Help children say in French whether or not their predictions were correct.

Oui, c'est exact.

Non, c'est faux.

57. Using equipment

✦ Show children how to use a bilingual dictionary, then challenge them to label their drawings of equipment used in an investigation – in French.

✦ After children have looked up translations for words naming and describing equipment, ask them to write the words in alphabetical order.

58. Researching famous French scientists

✦ Children use the internet to research a famous French scientist such as Louis Pasteur or Marie Curie (she was Polish but moved to France at the age of 24 and became a French citizen). Encourage them to find out the French for key words in their research.

les bactéries	bacteria
Il est né./Elle est née.	He was born./She was born.
la maladie	disease
le choléra	cholera

✦ Once children have researched their chosen scientist, invite them to take the 'hot seat' and answer questions posed by the class. Questions could include:

Where were you born?

Why are you famous?

How many children did you have?

What impact have you had on our lives today?

How old were you when you died?

Clap any children who can pose a question, or answer it, in French.

Fact file: Louis Pasteur

He was born on the 27th December 1822 in Dole, France.

He is best known for his breakthroughs in the causes and preventions of diseases.

He started his career demonstrating that organisms such as bacteria were responsible for souring wine, beer and milk.

He showed that bacteria could be removed by boiling and then cooling the liquid.

This process is now called pasteurization.

Pasteur then proved that bacteria come from the environment.

He helped the silk industry identify parasites that were affecting the silk worms.

He investigated the causes of diseases such as cholera, TB and smallpox and developed vaccines.

He is famous for working on a vaccine for rabies.

He died on the 28th of September 1895, a national hero.

Life processes and living things

Humans and other animals

59. Discussing nutrition

✦ Help children make a poster showing various foods in French and English. Talk together about the health benefits – and any downsides – of each food.

la salade	salad
les légumes	vegetables
les fruits	fruit
le poulet	chicken
un sandwich	a sandwich
les pâtes	pasta
une glace	an ice cream
un jus d'orange	orange juice
de l'eau	water
un café	coffee
un thé	tea
un yaourt	a yoghurt

✦ In discussing healthy food help children to express opinions about their food choices.

Les carottes sont bonnes pour moi.	Carrots are good for me.
Je n'aime pas le chou.	I don't like cabbage.
C'est bon pour la santé.	It is good for the health.
C'est mauvais pour la santé.	It is bad for the health.

60. Talking about teeth

✦ Revise numbers to 32 when working on teeth. A child with a full set has 20 teeth, and an adult with a full set has 32 teeth. Children could learn the French words for a tooth, and a dentist.

une dent   a tooth

un dentiste   a dentist

✦ Revise 'J'ai' and 'a' when talking about how many teeth people have.

J'ai vingt dents.

Mon père a trente-deux dents.

61. Talking about exercise

✦ Introduce words for hobbies and help children express their opinions of them.

J'adore le roller.

J'aime la danse.

Je n'aime pas le basket.

Je déteste le rugby.

✦ Teach children how to say 'faster' and 'slower' when they exercise then take their pulse rates.

plus vite   faster

plus lentement slower

62. Sorting skeletons

✦ Learn the names of some animals that have skeletons, and some that don't. Sketch animals, with or without skeletons as appropriate, and label them in French.

un humain	a human
un chien	a dog
un lion	a lion
un requin	a shark
une limace	a slug
un escargot	a snail

63. Growing up and growing older

✦ Establish how to ask how old someone is, and how to say your age.

Quel âge as-tu?

J'ai dix ans.

✦ Look at pictures of people at different stages in their life and guess their age.

Il a trente-cinq ans.

Elle a soixante-dix ans.

✦ Develop sentence work so children can explain how old their immediate family members are.

Ma mère a trente-huit ans.

Mon père a quarante ans.

Ma sœur a dix-sept ans.

Mon frère a dix ans.

Ma grand-mère a soixante-dix ans.

Mon grand-père a soixante-et-onze ans.

Green plants

64. Measuring temperatures

✦ Revise numbers with children as they read and record different temperatures. Help children respond to the temperatures they measure with a weather phrase.

Il fait chaud.

Il fait froid.

Il fait beau.

Il fait mauvais.

65. Naming plants

✦ When children label the parts of the plant they could add the name of their plant in French. Revise colours and word order in a simple phrase containing a noun and an adjective.

une rose rouge	a red rose
une jonquille jaune	a yellow daffodil
une campanule bleue	a blue bluebell

Variation and classification

66. Exploring minibeasts

✦ When children use pooters to collect animals, they can use a bilingual dictionary to find the name of the animal in French.

✦ Children can make detailed drawings of their creatures' bodies and label the different parts in French, revising numbers and parts of the body.

quatre jambes	four legs
une tête	one head
deux yeux	two eyes
deux oreilles	two ears
une bouche	one mouth

Living things in their environment

67. Talking about habitats

✦ Revise animals in French, then learn the names of some habitats.

✦
un lion	a lion
un poisson	a fish
un oiseau	a bird
un serpent	a snake
la jungle	the jungle
la mer	the sea
le désert	the desert
la fôret	the forest

✦ Combine these into sentences describing where each animal lives.

Un lion habite dans la jungle.

Un poisson habite dans la mer.

Un serpent habite dans le désert.

Un oiseau habite dans la fôret.

✦ Sing and mime the song 'Incy Wincy Spider' in French.

L'araignée Gipsy

L'araignée Gipsy
Monte à la gouttière
Tiens voilà la pluie!
Gipsy tombe par terre
Mais le soleil a chassé la pluie
L'araignée Gipsy
Monte à la gouttière …

68. Exploring feeding relationships

✦ Revise the verb *manger* and use it in a range of sentences.

L'oiseau mange le ver.   The bird eats the worm.

Le lion mange le zèbre.   The lion eats the zebra.

La chenille mange le chou.   The caterpillar eats the cabbage.

✦ Use a dictionary to draw and label as many types of green plant as possible.

Materials and their properties

Grouping and classifying materials

69. Sorting materials

✦ Hold up examples of conductors and insulators one at a time. Ask children whether the material conducts electricity. They must respond with 'Oui' or 'Non'.

✦ Do the same thing with materials that are, or are not, magnetic.

Changing materials

70. Learning about the water cycle

✦ Children could learn some words and phrases to describe the water cycle in French. Invite small groups to act out the cycle, holding large flashcards or give pairs smaller sets of the flashcards to order. Children then draw the cycle in their books.

le cycle de l'eau	the water cycle
le stockage d'eau dans les océans	holding of water in the oceans
le stockage d'eau dans l'atmosphère	holding of water in the atmosphere
le stockage d'eau dans la neige et la glace	holding of water in snow and ice
la précipitation	precipitation
l'évaporation	evaporation
la condensation	condensation

Physical processes

Electricity, forces and motion, light and sound

71. Talking science in French

✦ Help children to describe the brightness of a bulb.

C'est brillant.	It is bright.
C'est faible.	It is dim.

✦ When making a display about magnetic forces, help children to add the French versions of key words.

l'aimant	magnet
tirez	pull
poussez	push
attirez	attract
repoussez	repel

✦ Learn the verb 'voir' and some other simple vocabulary to talk about visible and invisible objects.

voir	to see
je vois	I see
tu vois	you see
il/elle voit	he/she sees
visible	visible
invisible	invisible
Je vois une fenêtre.	I can see a window.
Il voit une table.	He can see a table.
Elle voit l'ordinateur.	She can see the computer.
Je ne vois pas le vent.	I cannot see the wind.

The Earth and beyond

72. Learning about the planets

✦ Learn the names of the planets in French. Children could draw pictures of the planets, to scale, and label them.

le soleil	the Sun
Mercure	Mercury
Vénus	Venus
La Terre	Earth
Mars	Mars
Jupiter	Jupiter
Saturne	Saturn
Uranus	Uranus
Neptune	Neptune
Pluton	Pluto (now officially a dwarf planet)

✦ Get children to examine French translations of simple sentences about some of the planets. Ask them to use these as a model when drawing and describing their own invented planet.

Jupiter est une planète rouge.	Jupiter is a red planet.
Mars est une grande planète.	Mars is a big planet.
Mercure est une planète minuscule.	Mercury is a small planet.
Ma planète est marron et jaune.	My planet is brown and yellow.
Ma planète est rapide.	My planet is fast.

Design and Technology

Design and technology is a chance to compare cultural items. Children could design their object for a French pen pal, or to sell in a French shop. How could they make it appeal to the French market? Would they make it different if it was to be sold in England?

They can label their design, and list their resources in French. The cooking part of the DT curriculum is a fantastic opportunity to taste some French food and to try out some French recipes. Children can then design and make their own variations of these. Finally, their product can be evaluated in French, using key words and an appropriate tone of voice.

73. Developing, planning and communicating ideas

✦ Children could compare designed items, for example, their toys and the toys that children use in France, using the Internet to research this.

✦ If children have pen pals in France they could write and describe the design of their bread box/toy to them.

74. Working with tools, equipment, materials and components to make quality products

✦ Revise the names of classroom objects. Then encourage children to use the French words when asking another child to pass the ruler, or enquiring whether they have finished with the glue.

un crayon	a pencil
des ciseaux	the scissors
une règle	a ruler
la colle	the glue
le tissu	the fabric
le bois	the wood

75. Evaluating processes and products

✦ Use simple phrases to evaluate products.

C'est comment?	How is it?
C'est super!	It is great!
C'est bien.	It is good.
Comme çi comme ça./ *C'est pas mal.*	It is okay.
C'est nul.	It is bad.

76. Making brochures

✦ When children have finished making a product they can design a brochure advertising it to French children.

77. Making sandwiches

✦ If making sandwiches as part of a food project, help children to draw the ingredients and label them in French.

mon sandwich	my sandwich
le pain	the bread
le beurre	the butter
le thon	the tuna
le jambon	the ham
le fromage	the cheese
la salade	the salad

78. Trying out some French cooking

✦ One famous French dish is the Croque-Monsieur, a toasted ham and cheese sandwich. Another is the Quiche Lorraine, a traditional French dish named after the Lorraine region. This is a baked dish consisting of eggs and milk in a pie crust. It is traditionally made with a bacon filling, but you can add whatever you please.

✦ Children could make a Croque-Monsieur or a quiche, then write a recipe card to describe the process.

✦ Children could also make a typical English dish, and write out a recipe card to send to French pen pals.

Croque-Monsieur

POUR 4 PERSONNES
FOR 4 PEOPLE

INGRÉDIENTS
INGREDIENTS

8 tranches de pain de mie
8 slices of bread

8 grandes et fines tranches d'emmental
8 slices of emmental cheese

2 grandes tranches de jambon de Paris
2 slices of ham

50 g de beurre
50 g of butter

PRÉPARATION
METHOD

Coupez en deux chaque tranche de jambon, à la même taille que les tranches de pain de mie.

Cut each ham slice into two pieces, the same size as the bread.

Beurrez les huit tranches de pain. Déposez une tranche d'emmental et le jambon sur quatre d'entre elles. Recouvrez avec les autres tranches de fromage.

Butter the eight slices of bread. Place one piece of emmental and of ham on four of the pieces. Cover with the remaining slices of cheese.

Poivrez et posez les dernières tranches de pain beurrées par-dessus.

Season and put the remaining buttered bread slices on top.

Déposez-les sur une plaque chaude dans le four préchauffé à 220 °C. Faites-les dorer 10 minutes, dégustez accompagné d'une salade verte. Bon appétit!

Place on a heated baking tray in a preheated oven at 220 °C. Brown for 10 minutes and eat with a green salad. Enjoy your meal!

79. **Food tasting and evaluation**

✦ Children could taste samples of French food and evaluate it. They could put the samples in rank order from their favourite to their least favourite.

80. **Designing, making and evaluating**

✦ Children could design, make and evaluate a model of the Eiffel Tower as an extended task. Art straws work well for this.

The Eiffel Tower

The Eiffel Tower is Paris's most recognized icon.

The Eiffel Tower was designed by Gustave Eiffel and built for the World Exposition, held in Paris in 1889.

The Eiffel Tower is 312 m high.

It is built from 10 100 tons of iron.

There are 1 665 steps to the top of the Eiffel Tower.

An estimated 7 000 000 people visit the Eiffel Tower each year.

Information and Communication Technology

With the Internet and email it is now relatively easy to find out about, and communicate with, other countries. Children develop high order ICT skills as they progress through primary school and by Year 6 can use a wide range of tools and programs.

Children can record drama and role-play using camcorders, and use the clip in a PowerPoint presentation. A combination of ideas can be used by Year 6 children as an end of year project which could possibly be shared with secondary school teachers as part of their transition to Year 7.

81. Finding things out

✦ Children can use the internet to research aspects of French life and culture and compare it to their own. Or they could use it when learning about the geography of France, including rivers and mountains.

l'internet	the Internet
un site internet	a website
un moteur de recherche	a search engine

82. Developing ideas and making things happen

✦ Children can develop their mouse and keyboard control at the same time as practising their French vocabulary by using one of the many websites with games on.

✦ To help children when talking about the keyboard in French, ask a group to research and make a simple vocabulary poster

la souris	the mouse
le clavier	the keyboard
entrer	to enter
effacer	to delete
les lettres	the letters
les chiffres	the numbers

Exchanging and sharing information

83. Writing to pen pals

✦ Some schools set up links with partner schools in France. Children can email pen pals in their partner school and exchange information about their daily lives, their hobbies, their school ...

envoyer	to send
joindre un document	to attach a document
à	to
de	from
la boîte de réception	inbox
spam	spam
messages envoyés	sent messages

84. Making PowerPoint presentations

✦ Children can make PowerPoint presentations on a French topic such as Paris, French food, famous French people or a trip to France.

✦ Children can make a PowerPoint presentation to help teach younger children French vocabulary – for example, colours or animals.

85. **Word processing skills**

✦   Children can make an information leaflet based on their
     French learning for their parents. Encourage children
     to think carefully about the audience, and to choose
     content appropriately. Talk about ways of checking the
     quality of their work.

History

In history lessons children can learn about the culture and history of France. They can find out about the kings and queens, and learn about the end of the monarchy in France. The Second World War is an ideal subject for language links, as both Britain and France played very big parts.

You can label displays in French as well as English, with children using the context and some known words to extend their language learning.

Chronological understanding

86. Learning about kings and queens

✦ When children learn about a particular period in English history, challenge them to use the Internet to find out who was on the throne in France at that time.

Knowledge and understanding of events, people and changes in the past

87. Discussing the pros and cons of a monarchy

✦ Explain why there is no monarchy in France today, then invite children to a debate, where they take sides for monarchy or democracy.

Who rules France?

In 1789 the French people rebelled against, and overthrew, the monarchy; this significant event is now known as the French Revolution. The people felt that the king had too much power and treated the people unfairly and claimed their rights with the 'déclaration des droits de l'homme.'

Since then there has been no monarchy in France. Instead there is a president and a prime minister. The president is directly elected by the French people every five years. He/she is the head of state and has control over foreign policy and defence.

Every five years there are also parliamentary elections to choose a prime minister. The prime minister serves as head of government and is in charge of domestic policy and day-to-day governing.

Historical interpretation

88. Imagining a royal family

✦ Children draw a royal family and label the members using French.

le roi	the king
la reine	the queen
le prince	the prince
la princesse	the princess

Historical enquiry

89. Researching French history

✦ Children use a range of sources of information to research an important part of French history, such as the origins of Bastille Day.

✦ If children choose Bastille day, they can compare it to national days in Britain: St Georges Day in England, St Andrew's Day in Scotland, St Patrick's Day in Ireland and St David's Day in Wales. Suggest they plan how to celebrate the day in school.

✦ They could make a fact file to inform younger pupils.

✦ Provide children with a video camera to record them acting out an imaginary news report.

Bastille Day

Bastille Day is a French national holiday held on the 14th July every year. It commemorates a day over 200 years ago which marked the end of the monarchy in France and the beginning of the modern republic.

On the morning of July 14th 1789, a group of revolutionaries decided to attack the Bastille prison to get ammunition for their guns (ammunition was stored in the prison). The prison guards fired on them, and ended up killing hundreds of people.

The king's soldiers were so horrified by this that they refused to fight against the people and from then on, the revolution against the king was won.

A few years after this, in 1793, the king, Louis XVI, and his wife, Marie-Antoinette, were sent to their death by guillotine.

90. Researching the Second World War

✦ The Second World War is a useful topic for bringing French learning into the study of history.

✦ France and Britain played very important roles in the war, and it is a history topic that children usually find interesting and rewarding.

✦ As a reason for bringing French language into the topic, ask children to imagine that they are French children who are living in Britain during the war. Perhaps they were on a visit here when war was declared and their parents decided it was safer to stay in Britain than return to France.

91. Making statements about the war

✦ The teacher can read out statements about the war and about civilian life in wartime. Children respond with 'vrai' or 'faux'.

92. **Imagining evacuation**

✦ Follow a child through the process of evacuation, using simple French language. The child gets on a train, travels away from the city and the bombs, then arrives in the country to live with a strange family.

l'évacuation	the evacuation
le train	the train
la gare	the station
les bombes	the bombs
la campagne	the country

✦ Look together at pictures of children evacuatees and discuss their feelings.

Il est triste.	He is sad.
Il pleure.	He is crying.
Il est seul.	He is lonely.

✦ Some children may be able to put in order the story of an evacuation, written in simple French sentences. They may not recognize all of the words, but can use their skills of deduction.

93. **Learning about rationing**

✦ Children can learn about the foods that were rationed in Britain, and why. Explain that in France there was also rationing, and in some parts of France there were severe food shortages. Help children to use bi-lingual dictionaries to look up the French names for foods that were rationed.

Le beurre était rationné.

Butter was rationed.

Les pommes de terre, le poisson et les fruits n'étaient pas rationnés.

Potatoes, fish and fruit were not rationed.

94. **Sending messages**

✦ Give children the opportunity to learn words and phrases that could be used to send special messages – letters, telegrams, coded messages. Perhaps as a French evacuee living in Britain they could write to their mother.

Salut Maman!

Comment ça va? Tout va bien ici.

J'habite dans une maison avec une femme qui s'appelle Mary.

Il n'y a pas de bombes à la campagne.

À bientôt

Paul

Hi Mum!

How are you? Everything is good here.

I live in a house with a lady called Mary.

There are no bombs in the countryside.

See you,

Paul

---

95. **Digging for victory**

✦ In October 1939, the government began a campaign
to encourage people to grow their own vegetables in
gardens and allotments. Chickens, rabbits, goats and pigs
were kept in gardens and parks. Children could write
sentences about this, and illustrate them.

*Dans mon jardin il y a dix choux, vingt choux de
Bruxelles et quinze carrottes.*

In my garden there are ten cabbages, twenty
sprouts and fifteen carrots.

Douze cochons habitent dans le parc.

Twelve pigs live in the park.

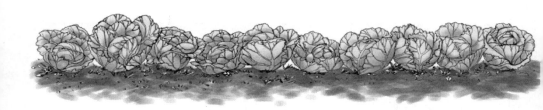

Geography

To complement French language learning children need to learn about the landscape of France, including its rivers and mountains. Make the most of any children who have visited France on holiday, asking them to talk about their experiences, and to bring in any souvenirs, postcards and photographs they may have of the country.

Knowledge and understanding of places

96. Discovering rivers

✦ Use an atlas to learn about where rivers are in France and label them on a map. Label the start and end of each river's journey.

Key rivers in France

Loire

Rhin

Dordogne

Seine

Garonne

Rhône

✦ Write down what you might see if you travelled on a 'bateau mouche' (open topped boat) through Paris, along the River Seine.

✦ Choose one river and use it to draw a labelled diagram that shows how rivers are formed.

la source	spring, source
le cycle de l'eau	water cycle
les précipitations	rainfall
la rivière	river
le ruisseau	stream
la colline	hill
la pente	slope
la montagne	mountain
la cascade	waterfall
la vallée	valley
le chenal	channel
le lac	lake
l'embouchure	mouth
l'érosion	erosion
la pollution	pollution
le paysage	landscape
raide	steep
serpenter	to meander

97. **Exploring mountains**

✦ Plot the mountains of France on a map.

Key mountains and mountain ranges in France

Mont Blanc

The Alps

The Massif Central

The Pyrenees

✦ Children research a mountain in France, for example Mont Blanc, and write a postcard home from a holiday there. Challenge them to provide a certain number of geographical facts.

Where are you?

How did you get there?

How high is the mountain?

What is the nearest town?

What language is everyone speaking?

What have you had to eat and drink?

---

98. **Naming countries in French**

✦ When working on the names and whereabouts of European countries, children can label them in French as well as English.

Les pays de L'Europe

la France	France
la Grande Bretagne	Great Britain
les Pays-Bas	Holland
l'Allemagne	Germany
la Belgique	Belgium
le Luxembourg	Luxembourg
l'Espagne	Spain
le Portugal	Portugal
le Danemark	Denmark
la Suisse	Switzerland
l'Autriche	Austria
la Turquie	Turkey

Art and Design

Studying French art and artists will provide many opportunities for using the French language. Children can look at a painting and respond with a sentence that you have modelled for them. They can try to create work in the style of a particular artist and comment on the results.

Evaluating and developing work

99. Giving opinions of art work

✦ Very simply, the children give their opinion of an artwork.

C'est super.	It's great.
C'est bien.	It's good.
Comme çi comme ça.	It's okay.
C'est nul.	It's bad.

Knowledge and understanding

100. Discussing colours

✦ Look at some paintings by French artists and comment on the colours in French.

Je vois la couleur bleue.	I can see the colour blue.
Il n'y a pas d'orange.	There is no orange.
J'aime la couleur violette.	I like the purple.

101. Examining clothing

✦ Children describe the clothes worn by people in a French painting or photograph. Encourage them to use the clothing to give an approximate date for the picture.

une grande jupe rouge	a big red skirt
une petite veste grise	a small grey jacket
il y a environ 50 ans	about 50 years ago

Music

Children enjoy singing and playing instruments. Teaching them traditional French songs can lead on to writing their own words for songs. They can also write songs to support younger children with their language learning. There is also the opportunity to learn about a famous French musician or composer, and to discuss and evaluate their style.

102. Listening and appraising

✦ Listen to the music of French musician Jean Michel Jarre. Draw the images that the music creates in your head. Use some French words to describe it.

rapide	fast
lent	slow
lourd	heavy
léger	light
électronique	electronic
l'instrument	instrument

Fact file: Jean-Michel Jarre

Jarre was born on the 24th August 1948, in Lyon, France.

He has three children called Emily, Barnaby and David.

He is a composer, performer and music producer.

His music is described as electronic, instrumental, New Age and ambient.

He plays the synthesizer and keyboard.

He is famous for organizing outdoor spectacles of his music, including lights, laser displays and fireworks.

He is in the 1997 *Guiness Book of Records* for the biggest concert ever with 3.5 million people watching at Moscow's 850th anniversary.

He has sold an estimated 80 million albums and singles worldwide.

103. Learning French songs

✦ Learn some French songs and their English translations.

Frère Jacques

Frère Jacques, Frère Jacques,
Dormez-vous? Dormez-vous?
Sonnez les matines; sonnez les matines
Din, din, don! Din, din, don!

✦ Children use vocabulary they have learnt to make up their own version of a song, using the same tune. For example, they could make up a colour song, using the tune for Frère Jacques.

Les couleurs

Bleu, bleu, marron; bleu, bleu, marron,
Vert, blanc, noir. Vert, blanc, noir.
Orange et violet; orange et violet,
Rose, rouge, jaune! Rose, rouge, jaune!

---

104. Creating a French mood

✦ Listen to some 'Paris Café' music while tasting French food. What mood does the music create and how does it achieve that?

✦ Children could follow up this activity by writing a postcard home to parents, pretending they are in a café in Paris. They describe where they are, what they can see, what they have eaten, how they feel, what they have visited in Paris.

Physical Education

Warm ups are an opportunity to use French as children respond to simple commands to prepare their bodies for exercise. Children can also learn about traditional French sports such as petanque, or research French sportspeople.

Breadth of study

105. Counting while you warm up

✦ Reinforce counting in French whilst warming up for PE.

✦ Skip and count in French.

✦ Throw the ball in pairs, taking it in turns to count.

✦ Do 25 star jumps together, counting them out loud.

106. Warming up in French

✦ Teach the children a simple warm-up using basic French vocabulary.

touchez	touch
frappez des mains	clap
sautez	jump
marchez	walk
plus vite	faster
plus lentement	slower

107. Running to the picture

✦ Put pictures of your current French topic in the corners of the hall: animals, colours, buildings, clothing ... Call out a word and children run to the corner where that picture is displayed.

108. Trying a traditional French sport

✦ Petanque is a version of boules. Players have two balls each and roll them towards a smaller ball, known as a jack in English and a cochonette in French. Plastic boules sets are quite cheap to buy. As four players share a set, eight sets is enough for a whole class to use. Look for video footage of French people playing petanque for children to watch before they play, and teach them some simple vocabulary to use as they play.

109. Learning about French sports people

✦ Enthuse the children by telling them about famous French sportspeople.

✦ football: Thierry Henry, Zinedine Zidane

tennis: Amélie Mauresmo

athletics: Marie-José Perec

✦ Play some traditional French playground games, such as this one, similar to 'What's the time, Mr Wolf?'

Un, deux, trois, soleil!

The catcher stands facing a wall. The other players stand about 20 m away, on a starting line, facing that person.

The aim of the game is to reach the wall and say 'Soleil' without the catcher seeing them move.

The catcher knocks three times on the wall, calling 'un, deux, trois.' This is the prompt for the other players to start moving towards the wall.

The catcher can at any time call 'Arrêt!' ('Stop!') and immediately turn around. Any players who are seen moving must go back to the starting line.

This process is repeated until one of the players reaches the wall and shouts 'Soleil.'

Religious Education

Children will enjoy learning about how festivals are celebrated in France, and having the opportunity to experience some typical French food. Children can learn about key religions in France to further develop their understanding of the wider world. You can say French prayers in assembly. Children can use the model prayer provided to adapt and write their own versions, using dictionaries for unknown words.

110. Using French during worship

✦　Use a French prayer in assembly.

Mon Dieu,	Dear God
Merci pour les fleurs,	Thank you for the flowers,
Merci pour les animaux,	Thank you for the animals,
Merci pour la famille et	Thank you for family and
les copains.	friends.
Amen.	Amen.

✦　Children use the above prayer as a model to write their own prayer in French, using a dictionary as necessary.

111. Exploring religion in France

✦ Teach children some basic facts about religion in France, using French words as appropriate.

Religion in France

France has traditionally been a Roman Catholic country and today approximately 80% of the population of France consider themselves Catholic. In reality, however, France is a deeply secular country, and the vast majority of these Catholics do not attend church regularly or ever.

About one million French people consider themselves to be Protestant. Protestants (then called Huguenots) were once severely persecuted by the French government.

Islam is another important religion in France. Many French Muslims are of North African decent – Africans came to France in large numbers during the 1950s and 1960s when France needed people to work in its factories and offices.

France has had a Jewish community since Roman times, however this was largely wiped out during the Middle Ages when Jews were persecuted and expelled. Many of the Jews in France today are recent immigrants from Morocco, Algeria and Tunisia.

112. Exploring festivals

✦ Talk with the children about French religious celebrations and compare them to those celebrations children themselves know about.

La Fête des Rois (the Holiday of the Kings)

This commemorates twelfth night, when the three kings are said to have arrived in Bethlehem; the celebration takes place on the first Sunday in January. It is traditional to eat a galette, which is a sweet, round cake with a fève or charm hidden within it. (Fève literally means broad bean, and originally the charm was just that.) Whoever gets the piece of cake with the charm is King or Queen for the day and gets to wear a crown.

une fève	*a broad bean/a charm*
un roi	*a king*
une reine	*a queen*
une couronne	*a crown*
une boulangerie	*a bakery*

Mardi Gras

Mardi Gras literally means 'fat Tuesday' and is a time of carnival. It falls on the day before Ash Wednesday; this means it is the last day before Lent, a 40-day period of fasting, ending on Easter Sunday, and so a good time to finish up any rich or luxurious foods.

In a typical carnival, people in elaborate costumes line the streets to watch processions and floats; there is usually much music, dance, food and drink.

un carnaval	*a carnival*
un costume	*a costume*
une fête	*a party*
un défilé	*a parade*

Pâques (Easter)

Easter is celebrated in France in much the same way as in Great Britain. Traditionally it was the bell that bought Easter eggs, but nowadays it is the Easter Bunny.

Joyeuses Pâques	*Happy Easter*
un oeuf de Pâques	*an Easter Egg*
un lapin de Pâques	*Easter bunny*
un poussin	*a chick*
un agneau	*a lamb*
une église	*a church*
une cloche	*a bell*

Noël (Christmas)

Christmas starts on the December 6th when Saint Nicholas' Day is celebrated. Many towns have carnival processions where Saint-Nicolas, as he is known in France, arrives and throws sweets to the children.

At Christmas dinner a bûche de Noël (*a chocolate log*) is served for pudding.

La Fête de Saint Nicolas	*Saint Nicholas' Day*
Joyeux Noël	*Happy Christmas*
un bonhomme de neige	*a snowman*
le Père Noël	*Father Christmas*
un cadeau	*a present*
un sapin	*a Christmas tree*

La Chandeleur (Candlemas)

Candlemas commemorates the day when the baby Jesus was presented to God in the Temple at Jerusalem. It is on the 2nd February. Lots of crêpes are eaten on this day.

une crêpe	*a pancake*
une crêpe au chocolat	*a chocolate pancake*
un œuf	*an egg*
le lait	*milk*
la farine	*flour*
le beurre	*butter*
le sucre	*sugar*

113. **Baking a galette**

In the first week of school in January, bake a galette with a fève inside (use a dried bean, not a hard charm). Present the galette with a crown on top. The person who receives the slice with the fève in it can be king or queen for the day and receive special treatment.

La Galette des Rois

INGRÉDIENTS

INGREDIENTS

500 g de pâte feuilletée

500 g puff pastry

1 haricot sec ou un bonbon mou

1 dry bean or a soft sweet

1 œuf

1 egg

175 g de pâte d'amande

175 g marzipan

une couronne en papier

a paper crown

PRÉPARATION

METHOD

Préchauffez le four à 200 °C.

Preheat the oven to 200 °C.

Graissez du papier sulfurisé.

Grease some baking paper.

Étalez la pâte sur 20 cm.

Roll out the pastry into a 20 cm round.

Étalez la pâte d'amande sur la pâte feuilletée.

Spread the almond paste on the pastry.

Cachez le haricot.

Hide the bean (anywhere in the filling).

Battez l'oeuf et étalez-le avec un pinceau à l'extérieur de la pâte.

Beat the egg and paint around the edges to seal the galette.

Étalez une nouvelle pâte sur 20 cm, placez-la sur la pâte d'amande.

Roll out another 20 cm piece of pastry and place over the almond filling.

Pressez les bords ensemble. Marquez la couche et dorez avec l'œuf.

Press the edges together and score the pastry. Glaze with the remaining egg .

Faites cuire au four pendant 25 minutes.

Bake for 25 minutes.

Servez avec la couronne au-dessus.

Serve with the crown on top.

114. Considering religious places

✦ Ask the children which religious buildings they know of locally. Discuss who goes there and why. Lead on to a discussion of other religious places children have heard of, and then talk about one or more of the places described below.

Some religious places in France

Sacre Coeur

This Roman Catholic church was completed in 1914. It is located at the highest point of Paris. It is famous for its dome which is open to tourists and has great views. There is also a garden for contemplation, with a fountain.

Notre Dame

This gothic cathedral is named for Mary, Jesus' mother ('notre dame' means 'our lady'). Construction began in 1163 and took nearly 200 years – it was finally completed in 1345. It is the seat of the Archbishop of Paris.

Lourdes

Lourdes is a small market town in south-western France. It is famous for the appearances of Mary, Jesus' mother, that Bernadette Soubirous is said to have seen in 1858. Lourdes has become a major place of Christian pilgrimage and miraculous healings are said to happen there. Millions of tourists and pilgrims visit each year.

Personal, Social, Citizenship and Health Education (PSCHE)

You can use French as a warm up in circle time. Children can use their knowledge of basic sentence work to describe themselves, or their friends, or to plot out the career path they would like to follow.

115. Using a parachute

✦ If you have access to the hall or a playground, parachutes are a fantastic way to have fun as a class and work as a team. Spread out the parachute on the ground and ensure that the class is evenly spaced around it, and holding on tightly, before lifting it up.

✦ Start by teaching simple instructions in French:

marchez à gauche	walk to the left
marchez à droite	walk to the right
arrêtez	stop
plus vite	faster
plus lentement	slower
levez le parachute	lift the parachute
baissez le parachute	lower the parachute

✦ Then play some games. Call out instructions in French.

Les chiffres (numbers)

Give each child a number from 1 to 5: un, deux, trois, quatre, cinq. When you call out a number, those children run round to take up a new position holding the parachute.

Le chat et la souris (cat and mouse)

Everyone holds the parachute stretched out at about waist height. Someone becomes the mouse and goes underneath. Someone else becomes the cat and goes on top. The rest of the class try to hide the mouse from the cat by moving the parachute up and down.

Le champignon (mushroom)

Everyone holds the parachute above their heads, then pulls it down behind their bottoms and sits down to form a 'mushroom' under which everyone is hidden. Once inside the mushroom you can count around the circle, or name colours in French.

116. Describing yourself

✦   Give children a picture of a French child and a piece of writing where the child describes him or herself. Children read the sentences carefully and then adapt them to describe themselves.

Salut! Je m'appelle Henry. J'ai dix ans.

J'ai une soeur qui s'appelle Mary, et deux frères qui s'appellent Sam et Dominic.

J'habite en Angleterre.

J'ai un hamster noir qui s'appelle Nibbles.

J'aime le bleu et l'orange.

Je fais de l'équitation.

Hi! My name is Henry. I am 10 years old.

I have one sister called Mary, and two brothers called Sam and Dominic.

I live in England.

I have a black hamster called Nibbles.

I like blue and orange.

I go horse riding.

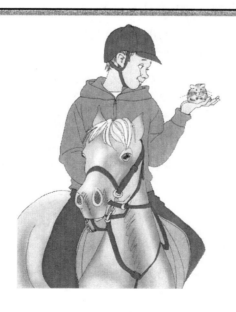

117. Thinking about the qualities of a good friend

✦ Children draw a good friend and write adjectives to describe them.

✦ Describing girls

Elle est:

sympa	nice
gentille	kind
bavarde	chatty
sportive	sporty

✦ Describing boys

Il est:

sympa	nice
gentil	kind
bavard	chatty
sportif	sporty

✦ Older children can write a phrase or sentence.

Ma copine s'appelle Lucy. Elle a neuf ans. Elle est sympa et bavarde.

My friend is called Lucy. She is 9 years old. She is nice and chatty.

Mon copain s'appelle Paul. Il a dix ans. Il est bavard et sportif.

My friend is called Paul. He is 10 years old. He is chatty and sporty.

118. Planning careers

Children discuss in pairs what they would like to be when they grow up, then draw their choice and label it in French.

✦ Older children could write some sentences.

I would like to be a vet.

Je voudrais être vétérinaire.

I like animals.

J'aime les animaux.

I am a hard worker.

Je suis travailleur/travailleuse.

119. Rewarding good behaviour

Make your reward chart in the shape of the Eiffel Tower. Children colour sections as a reward for good behaviour. When they reach each of the two cafes, and then the top, reward the class in some way.

120. Circle time

Use French words and sentences as a warm up in circle time. Everyone takes a quick turn to say something in French before the main part of the session begins. One day ask for favourite colours, another day ask for names of brothers, sisters or friends, and so on. Match the vocabulary work to your current topic in French, or use the time to reinforce a question that children find tricky.

Extending Language Learning

A crucial part of the modern foreign languages curriculum is developing children's knowledge of the wider world. They will learn about the country of France and its culture, alongside learning the language. They might discuss how to travel there, how long the journey would take, and where they could stay if they visited.

They should learn about the people, their customs and traditions, and compare these to their own. They should be encouraged to think about French and British stereotypes and to challenge them.

Children should also be given opportunities to learn about other countries around the world – it may surprise them to know that there are dozens of countries where French is either the main language or is widely spoken.

Learning a language can be very exciting for children. After a language day or other session, they often have clear ideas about what they would like to do next. Listen to the children and, as far as possible, use their ideas. We followed a theme called 'Round the World', which was first suggested by a child, and we enjoyed developing it and experiencing it with the whole of the key stage. Make language learning fun and the learning will take place, to a high standard, becoming firmly embedded in the children's minds.

121. **Having a French Day**

French Days are an ideal way to learn more about France and to enthuse both staff and children. The class, or the whole school, spends the day completing four or five activities that cross the curriculum. They could also taste and evaluate some French food. Plenty of ideas can be found earlier in this book.

- ✦ Encourage children and staff to come dressed in the colours of the French flag.
- ✦ Listen to some music by a French composer.
- ✦ Learn a French song, and some actions, to perform together in assembly. Children can copy out the words and decorate them to show they understand the lyrics. Younger children can just copy out the chorus, or illustrate words that have been provided.
- ✦ Learn about a French artist, and complete some artwork in their style.

✦ Play board games using French vocabulary. Remind children to say the number on the dice out loud in French, and to count in French, as they move around the board.

Tu voudrais jouer?	Would you like to play?
à ton tour	your turn
à mon tour	my turn
tu as gagné	you win
j'ai gagné	I win

✦ Each year group can record their experiences of the French Day using a different kind of text. Give children a checklist of the features appropriate to their text type. At the end of the session use the same list when conducting some peer assessment.

Year 3 draw and label pictures, focusing on presentation.

Year 4 write a diary.

Year 5 write a letter.

Year 6 write a newspaper report.

122. Having a French café

✦ Either as part of the French Day, or as a separate activity, dedicate one room to being a café for a day. Children ask for their food and drink in French, and listen to French music as they enjoy their food.

> *Merci, Madame/Mademoiselle/Monsieur.*
>
> Thank you, Madame/Miss/Sir.
>
> *Je voudrais une baguette et du fromage, s'il vous plaît.*
>
> I would like a baguette and some cheese, please.
>
> *Je voudrais de la brioche, s'il vous plaît.*
>
> I would like some brioche, please.
>
> *Je voudrais un croissant, s'il vous plaît.*
>
> I would like a croissant, please.
>
> *Je voudrais un jus d'orange, s'il vous plaît.*
>
> I would like some orange juice, please.
>
> *Je voudrais un chocolat chaud, s'il vous plaît.*
>
> I would like a hot chocolate, please.
>
> *Merci, Madame/Mademoiselle/Monsieur*
>
> Thank you, Madame/Miss/Sir.

✦ Children could make place mats as a way of revising the words for types of fruits and vegetables. They divide their place mat in half, and label the halves *J'aime* and *Je n'aime pas*. They choose which side of the mat to draw and label different foods.

✦ Locate your café in Paris and put up pictures of key places in Paris. Afterwards children could write a postcard home describing their visit to the café.

✦ Locate your café in Cannes, during the Film Festival.
Serve 'champagne' (clear lemonade) and canapés.
Children could write diary entries describing what they
have eaten, and the films and celebrities they have seen.

Festival de Cannes

✦ Locate your café in any city or town that is relevant to
the children. Talk about how to travel there, find the
town on a map, discuss the climate ... .

123. Learning about other Francophone countries

◆ Spend a half day learning about a different country where French is spoken, for example, Haiti, Senegal or Belgium.

◆ Dress in the colours of the country's flag. Draw or paint the flag, or make a flag from fabric scraps or coloured paper.

◆ Listen to the country's national anthem and describe it.

◆ Taste some traditional food or drink, learn about a famous person, find the country on a map or globe, explore its history … .

Ideas for countries

Haiti

Find Haiti on a map of the Caribbean. Try to pronounce some of the place names.

Find out about its recent history.

Find out about its past: Haiti was the first independent nation in Latin America and the first black-led republic.

Senegal

Find Senegal on a map (look in the 'bulge' of Africa).

Find out about the climate there: desert in the north and a hot, wet, tropical south.

Talk about the slaves that used to be taken from Senegal during the 17th and 18th centuries to work in the Americas and Europe.

Belgium

Find Belgium on a map of Europe. Talk about how you would get there from England or from France.

Find out about some famous Belgium people, such as Hergé, creator of Tintin.

Taste some Belgian chocolate.

124. Planning a British Day for French children

✦ After experiencing a French Day, children could plan a British Day for a French visitor.

✦ Children could choose what British food and drink to offer, make some posters about famous people or famous landmarks, choose some music by British composers … .

✦ Arrange for a real French visitor if possible; otherwise ask another friendly adult (perhaps a school governor) to take on a French persona for the day and come to sample the delights of the school's British Day.

125. Linking older and younger classes

✦ Consider pairing up classes so that older children work with younger children, passing on their knowledge and expertise. Children can pose simple questions in French, or play flashcard games to reinforce understanding of key vocabulary.

✦ Older children can make books, designed to suit the age and language ability of the younger children. Discuss with the writers what vocabulary is suitable, how many words to put on a page, how heavily illustrated the book needs to be, and so on.

✦ Children could write the book about themselves, or base it on a famous character. If pairing individuals, the older child can write a simple book about the younger child, all in French.

✦ A short book could use this format.

Page number	Topic	Possible structure
1	Name	Je m'appelle ...
	Age	J'ai ... ans.
2	Location	J'habite à ...
3	Family	J'ai ... soeur(s) et ... frère(s).
4	Pets	J'ai ...
5	Favoured activities	J'adore ...
		J'aime ...
		Je n'aime pas ...
6	Blurb	(written in English) author, price, barcode, ISBN number

✦ Spread this work over several weeks, perhaps as a project for the final half term of the year. If you choose, you can laminate the books and spiral-bind them.

✦ Children can read their books to the younger children they were designed for. Either the younger children can take them home, or the books can be displayed in the class or school library for use during quiet reading sessions.

126. Designing your own country

✦ Challenge groups of children to design their own country. They will need to decide where their country is, how it is governed and what language(s) are spoken there.

✦ Ask them to design a flag and write a national anthem to set to music (or borrow a tune from another song).

✦ Each child can draw a picture of a famous landmark and write about it.

✦ Ask them to design a currency and each draw a market stall showing different local produce priced in the local currency.

✦ Display information about each group's country and have a session where children talk about their country to the rest of the class.

Index

Index